HOW TO HANDLE DIVORCE:

The Effective And Proven Methods To Deal With Breakups and Heartbreaks

Michael R. Clary

Table of Contents

Chapter 1

Breaking up in Relationships

HOW DO BREAKUPS OCCUR?

Romantic partners frequently commit to one another by moving in together, setting up a specific amount of time each week for one another, or pledging not to see anyone else. When one or both of the partners decides they no longer want to keep these promises, relationships frequently end.

Sometimes only one party wants to end the relationship, even though a couple may both agree to do so. When the other partner does not want the relationship to end, this can be stressful and hurtful. Sometimes one spouse would cut off communication with the other and vanish to indicate the end of a relationship. Because it leaves the other partner feeling unsatisfied and the relationship status unknown, this manner of

ending a relationship can be especially unpleasant and difficult.
Depending on how the parties involved felt about the relationship, a breakup may be viewed as positive or negative. Even though the relationship was difficult, one or both partners may regret the breakup but believe it was for the best.

This realization may nevertheless create emotional distress. Unconcern or ambivalence may also be experienced upon a relationship's demise. In general, short-term, casual relationships are simpler to end and move on from than long-term, committed ones.

POSSIBLE REASONS FOR BREAKUPS

Many factors can lead to a breakup. Sometimes it's obvious when a relationship isn't going well: Abuse on either a physical or emotional level, an affair, or just general discontent are all indications of a bad relationship. It can also be challenging to decide whether to end a relationship. While a relationship may be enjoyable and momentarily satisfying, if it does not appear to be going anywhere and one or both partners want to stay in it for the long haul with the possibility of cohabitation, marriage, or children, it may be best to move on. However, ending a relationship when nothing is genuinely wrong might be challenging.

Relationships can also terminate when partners come to terms with having different priorities or values. These values may have been different at the start of the relationship or they may have evolved as the two persons grew as a couple and as individuals. It can be challenging to be open and honest with a dating partner about these situations for fear of upsetting that person. Sometimes one partner may develop affection for someone else or just lose interest in and attractiveness to the other person.

Even though two people have affection for one another and enjoy doing particular things together, sometimes their personalities are just incompatible. When a relationship doesn't work out and the partners find it increasingly difficult to enjoy their time together or feel thrilled about spending time together, they may decide that ending the relationship is best for both of them.

STARTING A BREACH

When one is ready to move on, emotionally withdrawing from a relationship may seem easier to do than starting a painful dialogue about ending it. However, as this tactic could ultimately bring more complication and suffering, it might be advisable to talk about the split as soon as possible. It can be helpful to carefully evaluate the reasons why a breakup could be preferable before starting the conversation so that these reasons can be conveyed to the other person openly and sincerely. Another justification for delaying the start of a breakup is the potential for the other person to react negatively. In this situation, anticipating possible negative responses may be beneficial and may also increase sensitivity.

Managing a breakup

According to a study in the journal Social Psychological & Personality Science, talking about a breakup and taking into account possible causes is frequently beneficial: Regaining one's sense of self via reflection could make it simpler to go on.

Relationships are an important part of life, and to move on, it is usually necessary to accept both their significance and the grief and sadness that comes with their loss. After a breakup, concentrating on self-care may be beneficial and speed up the healing process. Healthy eating, getting enough sleep, staying active, abstaining from potentially harmful behaviors like excessive drinking or drug use, and accepting support and care from family and friends are all likely to promote healing and enhance one's outlook.

Even while a breakup might cause emotions of shame or inadequacy, it can also be beneficial to reflect on one's development and the lessons—positive or negative—learned from the relationship. Knowing why a relationship did or did not work out can help you avoid making the same mistakes in the future.

Even a difficult split can result in growth. After a breakup, a period of loneliness can lead to personal development and discovery. New interests may have emerged, and priorities, values, and life goals may all have changed. Even though it may be challenging, accepting that interests can still be shared even after a relationship has ended may be beneficial for the healing process. It may be challenging to enjoy a hobby you once did with an ex-spouse.

Mental health and breakdowns

A breakup can be traumatic, and various factors, such as the following, may influence how emotionally heavy it is:

the duration of the partnership.

The future goals that each partner in the couple had.

the level of dedication to the partnership.

how content the relationship was before it ended.

Which spouse would like to continue the relationship?

Whether there was adultery, abuse, or another terrible reason why the partnership ended.

When a relationship ends, people occasionally refer to themselves as "broken-hearted," and the process of grieving a relationship is quite similar to grieving other losses. When a short-term relationship ends, a person could feel OK after only a few days, but when a long-term relationship ends, it might take months or years to truly grieve.

The amount of time it takes to get over a breakup can vary greatly. Because more people are living together permanently, a breakup can frequently resemble a divorce and create intense emotional distress because it destroys shared friendships, divides shared possessions, and occasionally raises custody questions.

Sometimes after a breakup, a couple will get back together, continue to have sex or stay in touch as friends for some time. Even though some individuals might view reconciliation favorably, research indicates that "on-again, off-again" couples frequently have lower levels of relationship satisfaction.

Situational depression frequently results from breakups, and some people experience suicidal thoughts as a result of their breakups. People frequently seek the assistance of therapists and other mental health specialists to deal with any unresolved emotions they may be experiencing following a breakup.

ASSISTANCE WITH BREAKUPS

When a relationship ends, especially a serious one, it can cause tension, anxiety, and depression. Whatever the circumstance, when a relationship ends, a person may feel sad, angry, bewildered, or in some other way emotionally affected. Even the partner who desired or started the separation may be experiencing this inner anguish.

A therapist or counselor can frequently be a supportive, beneficial part of the healing process when a breakup results in overwhelming, difficult-to-manage feelings, interferes with the ability to carry out daily tasks, or influences the reevaluation of one's life path, especially when conditions like depression, low self-esteem, grief, or posttraumatic stress develop after a breakup.

A person can address any emotions or problems they are having in therapy and look into coping mechanisms. An individual can come to terms with the breakup of the relationship and handle any shame or self-blame they may be feeling with the aid of a therapist. After a breakup, a therapist can also assist in treating depression and suicidal thoughts.

Chapter 2

Grieving Marriage Divorce

Although grieving a divorce can seem like a solitary experience, help is available, so you are not alone.

Numerous feelings, including sadness, relief, loneliness, rage, and even bereavement, can be triggered by divorce. Grief is a typical emotion to feel after a marriage ends, even though many people only link it with the loss of a loved one.

Grieving after a divorce can be difficult, but with time, support, and coping mechanisms, you can learn how to set your sadness apart and move on to this new phase of your life.

Why grieving a divorce could feel lonely

Grieving a divorce can be particularly challenging since you could feel like you're going through it alone.

Even though divorce no longer carries the stigma it once did, you could still feel guilty or inadequate. Your grieving may become more complicated by these emotions, which can also exacerbate any feelings of isolation or loneliness.

Because there aren't any customary grieving rituals like there are when a loved one passes away that friends and family can accompany you through, grieving a divorce can be exceptionally difficult.

For instance, mourning rituals like wakes and funerals allow the bereaved individual to share their pain with others when someone they love passes away.

A person who has lost a loved one is frequently expected by society to require special care and respect. To aid a person after a loved one passes away, it has been customary to provide meals, time off work, and other accommodations.

Although the intensity of your sadness may be similar, it is unusual to receive these gestures during a divorce. This does not imply that your loved ones don't care about you. They might simply be unsure of how to help you at this moment.

Knowing enfranchised grief

Many persons going through a divorce may have disenfranchised grief as a result of this lack of recognition.

This phrase was created by bereavement specialist Kenneth Doka in his book "Disenfranchised Grief: Recognizing Hidden Sorrow." When someone has a loss that isn't typically publically acknowledged, lamented, or socially supported, they may experience disenfranchised grief.

This phrase describes any postdivorce pain you might feel since, when a marriage fails, friends and neighbors frequently don't emerge from hiding with casseroles and condolences.

To let your loved ones know that you need extra assistance during this time, it may be helpful to express your grief to them directly.

How long does mourning after a divorce last?

How long it will take to recover after a divorce cannot be predicted with any degree of precision. In terms of how it impacts you or a loved one going through it, there is therefore no right or incorrect response.

Similar to how grieving a death takes time, so does grieving a divorce. Like the five stages of grieving a death or loss, you'll likely go through a succession of five stages. The phases could consist of:

Denial. A brief period of denial, which occurs frequently in the early stages of the mourning process, might lessen the blow of the original loss.
Anger. You will frequently experience a flurry of emotions throughout a divorce, including anxiety and pain. These feelings are frequently covered up by anger, but they can also spur you on to do so.
Bargaining.

Negotiating during a divorce may be a helpful step that enables you to determine if the marriage has genuinely ended. Counseling, couples retreat, or even just making pledges to each other to act differently in the future can all be used as types of bargaining during a divorce.
Depression. Usually, there is a brief period of depression after denial, rage, and bargaining. It accompanies the realization

that the marriage is gone and is an emotional admission of the possibility of sadness and regret.
Acceptance. When you've fully processed the divorce, acceptance usually happens as the last stage. You may usually leave at this point and begin building a new life for yourself.

The five phases of mourning are still often experienced, although many specialists believe they are out of date. You might not go through all the stages in order, just like when you are grieving the loss of a loved one. It's okay if some last longer than others.

Consider talking to friends or getting professional assistance if you feel stuck in a phase so you can process your emotions.

How to move past grief following divorce

Although moving past grief after divorce might be difficult, time and coping mechanisms can help you do so.

Try to be forgiving of yourself.
You'll probably respond in ways that surprise you, and you might experience unanticipated feelings. Remember that a divorce is likely to cause you to experience several significant losses. It's acceptable and even expected to experience a variety of emotions, including unexpected ones.

It's not necessary to always be well organized. Try to be patient with yourself and accept that it can take some time before you feel like yourself again.

Participate in a ceremony of grieving.
Grief and death-related rituals have been present in the earliest cultures. Funerals and wakes are just two examples of rituals and ceremonies.

According to a 2021 study, rituals can help those who are grieving by allowing them to remember a lost loved one, let go of a traumatic event, and envision themselves moving on to their next chapter of life.

A ritual in the context of divorce may then assist you in remembering your marriage, letting go of the pain and losses connected to it, and reinventing yourself as you move into a new stage of your life.

Even while there are no widely practiced ceremonial rites to follow a divorce, more people are discovering other methods to accept the loss and the change.

Some rituals related to divorce might be:

Leaving a letter behind
journaling about your grieving process once a week

making a list of the things you are getting and losing before burning your wedding dress
organizing a divorce party and creating a memory box
On the anniversary of your divorce, light a candle (or marriage)
Think about getting assistance

Even though it might feel like it, you are not alone. During the procedure, you can rely on friends or family for love and support. Even while they might not be able to fully get how you're feeling, they can nevertheless provide you support and sympathy.

Making a list of one to three persons who say they'll be there for you in an emergency may prove useful. You may rely on these folks for help whether they are friends, family members, or professionals.

Regardless of whether you have a strong network of friends or family to lean on, getting expert assistance could be a wise move. To help you through the mourning process and get past any potential feelings of loneliness, talk therapy and group therapy can be helpful resources.

You may even give self-help options some thought. For instance, a 2019 study discovered that after taking part in an online self-help program for three months, divorced and bereaved individuals had lower levels of sadness, melancholy, stress, embitterment, and loneliness than a control group.

Finding the techniques that are most effective for you may take some time. Use a variety of options, such as talking to friends, reading self-help books, and joining a support group, to make you feel like you have strong support coming from all angles.

Grief Resources for divorce

You're not alone, and there are tools available, even though societal conventions may not always give divorce the same respect they do to other events that lead to grief. These examples could be helpful:

DivorceCare.org is a company that connects people going through a divorce with support groups and offers services.
Men's Divorce: A website sponsored by a lawyer that provides educational resources, information, and assistance in finding legal counsel.

Woman's Divorce is a program offered by lawyers that assists in bringing together ladies going through a divorce with those who have already gone through or are going through a divorce.
Going forward
You are not alone in your pain if you are going through a divorce and find yourself crying. The most accessible coping mechanisms for divorce grieving include a

combination of mourning customs, expert assistance, and sympathy from friends and relatives.

Throughout this period, try to be gentle to yourself. Even though you can feel out of control and overtaken by your feelings, know that you are doing the best you can and that you will get through this.

Chapter 3

Connecting back to life

Breakups can be difficult. After a divorce, it can be challenging to end a relationship or move on. You might feel powerless, angry, hurt, or rejected. But there is hope at the end of the road. To manage these difficult feelings, you might employ a variety of tactics.

Your recovery process might not follow a straight line, and your discomfort might not go away right away. There will be numerous phases and times of adjustment, just like with any loss. It's crucial to keep moving and enjoy the journey. It's important to comprehend some of the emotions and phases that could appear.

Here are some suggestions to aid with the healing process:

Recognize your feelings. Long-term recovery depends on you allowing yourself to experience all of your emotions. Even though it could be awkward to express your negative feelings, doing so is necessary for the healing process to begin.

Discussion on it. You may find it beneficial to discuss your divorce with a qualified professional as you proceed. They can also provide you with useful guidance regarding the particulars of your divorce. You can concentrate on grieving the breakdown of your marriage by splitting the load of logistics.

Create effective coping mechanisms. When you're not feeling your greatest, the capacity to control your intense emotions can be quite useful. Try to adopt compassionate, uplifting self-care practices.

Becoming a good co-parent requires learning new skills. If you share children with your ex-spouse, you must now decide how to raise them in light of the situation. Children must be taken into account because this is a condition that will last a lifetime.

Stop getting stuck. When you feel yourself slipping into a state of despair, anxiety, or resentment, get assistance. Suffering alone can be harmful and steer you in the wrong direction.

Beware of desperation. You can get to the point where you feel driven to make things right with your ex-spouse. This might not be the best course of action for you, your partner, or your family in your particular circumstance.

Prevent a harsh rebound. Fear of becoming unlovable or of never experiencing love again may encourage you to look for a new partner. You may create connections based on love, not fear if you resist this urge and stay rooted in your recovery process.

Utilize all the tools at your disposal. You may find great resources for yourself in books, internet resources, religious activities, or any support organization for people who share your interests. Make sure to investigate and verify the organizations, books, or other resources you are thinking about.

Be aware that there is always hope. The road to getting over your divorce may not be easy. But constantly remember that you are moving forward and that recovery is possible.

Give yourself a pass. You might not be performing at your best at this moment. It's possible, that you won't be as effective at work or present as a friend. Everyone is susceptible to these things. Give yourself some time to rest and recover.

Ensure your well-being. Give yourself the gift of nutritious food and energizing exercise. As much as you can, maintain your regimen. Avoid making important life decisions. Refrain from abusing alcohol and drugs severely.

Break any bad habits you and your spouse have developed. Disengage from conversations if they start to turn into arguments. Leave the room or disconnect the phone.

Join forces with your interests. Spend some time getting back into your hobbies. This can resemble signing up for a softball team or taking a painting lesson. Whatever it may be, remember to have fun.

How to Discuss the Divorce with Your Children

It could be challenging to discuss the divorce with your children if you have any. There are many various ways to communicate with your kids and ease their adjustment to the new circumstances in your home. The following may be some of these tactics:

Leave them alone. Boost your kids' confidence. Attend to their worries and sentiments. Tell them what they need to know lovingly, the whole truth.

Ensure stability Keep up your children's regular schedules and routines during this period of adjustment in your family's life. Giving them security and comfort can feel quite firmly rooted in them.

Be constant and steadfast. Speak with your ex-spouse in advance about issues like house rules, discipline, and family values because your kids may spend time at both homes.

Allow your kids to rely on you. Make an effort to demonstrate to your kids that you are dependable, honest, and consistent so that they will feel comfortable confiding in you. Try not to express your emotions about the divorce, nevertheless, in too much detail.

Keep your kids apart from divorce. Be discreet about the processing you perform with your ex-spouse or by yourself. Avoid arguing with your ex-spouse and refrain from using your kids as spies or messengers.

.

Chapter 4

Learning from Divorce

Divorce Can Teach You Important Lessons About Love, Marriage, and Relationships.

There is a lot to learn about marriage, love, and relationships. You might not anticipate learning lessons about all three through a divorce. Divorce lessons are ones you won't ever forget since they have such a profound effect on you.

Even if life after divorce isn't always ideal, it can still be preferable to an unhappy marriage. One of the many advantages of divorce is that it allows you to appreciate your newfound freedom. Divorce, in particular for women, can teach them important life lessons while also making them wonder who they are or what love is.

Divorce, however, does have an impact on your life, whether it's through having to relearn how to live alone, figuring out how to get past the past, or just getting used to being by yourself. However, there are good reasons for divorce as well, including unhappiness, a developing disconnection, a loss of love, or infidelity.

The following are significant lessons that divorce teaches you about love, marriage, and relationships:

There will be no change in your companion. In other words, a cat cannot be transformed into a dog. Love is simply insufficient to drastically alter someone's fundamental makeup and upbringing.

For instance, if you fall in love with a reserved person and you depend on displays of affection to make you feel safe, you'll experience chronic dissatisfaction. These disparities most likely will cause love feelings to deteriorate over time and reduce constructive interactions in your partnership.

Instead of attempting to "repair" your partner, you should concentrate on bettering your own life.
I discovered the hard way that many people stay in unhealthy relationships out of an underlying desire to alter their partner rather than confront their difficulties.

This trend is frequent, and partners frequently continue in severely dysfunctional relationships to their own cost, say codependency and relationship experts.

The pleaser/fixer (codependent) and the taker/controller (narcissist), he writes, "need two opposed but distinctly balanced partners for the fundamentally flawed 'codependency dance'."

Commit to changing some of your unattractive traits instead of focusing your energy on trying to change your partner because we are all imperfect in some manner. You won't have a good, non-dysfunctional relationship until then, and only then.

Contraries are drawn to one another but rarely stay that way.
Rosenberg defines opposites as "human magnets" who are drawn to one another inexorably by their opposite "magnetic field," rather than by their conscious choices or intentions.

According to him, such partners with complimentary magnetic roles are pulled to one another and locked into a relationship that is practically impossible to avoid or escape from.

Due to the passionate nature of their relationship magnetism, he proposes that opposites-attracting couples are impervious to divorce — unless one spouse makes a healthier change and the other one doesn't follow.

This frequently occurs over time as people develop and change.

It's not a good idea to enter an intimate relationship too quickly.
Consider going very, very slowly. Despite the temptation, many individuals experience to move relationships ahead quickly, slowing things down will allow you to get to know your partner more fully.

When we take the time to get to know someone, our chances of discovering the reality of the relationship rise.

She suggests, "Many people engage in sexual activity before they are ready, which can cause potential problems to go unnoticed until much later in the relationship. I frequently witness this. Date. Talk. Get to know each other deeply."

One or two remarks about how quickly you were moving may have been made by your friends and family, but they weren't being sarcastic; they were merely trying to protect you.

I was surprised by many of our differences because, in my situation, I had only known my ex for less than a year at the time we became engaged and married.

You can go on if you practice forgiveness. Forgiveness in a relationship is different from tolerating the harm that has been done to you. However, it will enable you to continue living your life.

Recognize that most individuals try their best and make an effort to have more patience with them. This does not imply that you condone your partner's cruel behavior.

Simply said, you become more grounded and grant them less control over you.

Healthy relationships require both parties to adopt a mindset of acceptance and forgiveness toward minor setbacks that occur every day. We are all fallible, after all. Try to let go of minor irritations and avoid letting resentment have a big impact on you.

Generally speaking, problems don't go better by being swept under the rug.
Discuss important relationship concerns openly and honestly. Make careful, to be honest about your worries. Respectfully express your opinions, feelings, and wishes.

Couples should be sensitive and avoid letting angry sentiments grow because doing so might lead to resentment. Examine your assumptions and negative thoughts on holding onto hurt feelings.

You no longer need to harbor resentment after hearing your partner's side of the story and short discussing it with them.

Accept accountability for your contribution to the quarrel or disagreement.
The dynamics of the relationship can be altered by one person's capacity to do this.

The response of one individual will alter the other's brain waves."

So, when it's appropriate, apologize to your partner. This will support forgiveness, affirm their sentiments, and let the two of you go on.

Love is insufficient. Even if you didn't purposefully offend your partner, saying you're sorry can help the situation. If couples are unable to discuss the unpleasant feelings that result from unsolved disputes, resentment gradually grows over time.

Create a "Hurt-Free Zone" rule.
This phrase, which was invented by novelist David Akiva, designates a time when criticism is prohibited. Couples typically feel less defensive and less hurt and rejected without it.

Your priority right now should be to stop engaging in the most harmful negative communication and to dial back your negative feelings for three to four weeks."

Permit yourself to be exposed.
While independence and self-sufficiency can help you weather life's storms, they can also rob you of real closeness. Partners need to be able to rely on one another and feel wanted and valued for the assistance they provide for a relationship to be healthy.

The idea of needing someone can be dreadful if you've already been let down.

Although it can make you feel exposed and vulnerable, being open with your partner is the most crucial component of a secure, passionate connection. A warning sign is if you find it difficult to be vulnerable with your partner.

Gain confidence in your judgment.
You may need to pay heed to your inner voice or intuition if you frequently find yourself stating things like, "I knew things were horrible and I should have terminated it earlier."

Breaking up with someone does not make you a failure. Instead, it most likely signifies that it simply wasn't the best choice for you.

Says Davin "Because we want a relationship, we frequently ignore warning signs. We leave after donning our rose-colored glasses. Trust your instinct and throw the glasses away."

In conclusion, I don't look back on my past or regret getting divorced one bit. Even if my divorce permanently altered me, the lessons I acquired from it were worthwhile. But as a reminder of the things I've learned, I'll always have this list handy.

Whatever your divorce-related reasons, you deserve to be happy. To assist you move on as you navigate a new life after divorce and find the sort of love that enables you to be your best self and accept everything life has to offer, I hope these lessons will be helpful to you.

Chapter 5

Life After Divorce

Similar to a marriage, divorce frequently causes significant life changes.

A new house, an empty house, or even quieter meals can result from the procedure alone. Your co-parenting schedule may need you to spend days without your kids for the first time if you have kids.

You might go through a complex jumble of emotions, ranging from betrayal and grief to fury or even relief, as you start to get used to the new structure of your life.

Simply said, divorce can drastically alter your life. It might be a big benefit to remember that divorce doesn't spell the end of your life as you start to rebuild yourself. Instead, it denotes a fresh start.

An important first step to successfully navigating the post-divorce period is taking care of your mental and physical needs. The pointers listed below provide a place to start.

Adopt acceptance

Most people don't get married with the expectation that they will eventually divorce. Even though divorce is prevalent, you might be completely certain your marriage will endure.

Therefore, it could be a surprise when your marriage dissolves.

It's normal to feel regret, wish things had gone differently, and contemplate whether there was anything you could have done to stop it. Additionally, you can experience some perplexity and even denial as you struggle to accept the divorce.

But despite these very legitimate feelings, the marriage has ended.

Although some ex-spouses may remarry, divorce is typically a rather permanent break. Moving ahead and healing can both be hampered by holding on too firmly to the past or the idealized future.

Therefore, when you start to notice your thoughts moving in the direction of:

If only I'd...
"But our chemistry was great,"
"How could they discard everything?
"

Instead, attempt to recollect:

"The divorce took place, and there is no going back on that."
Even if things don't go according to plan, I can still be happy and at peace with myself.
It's normal to take some time to become accepted, so don't worry if you do. The most

important thing is to be nice to yourself as you adjust to your loss.

Give yourself room to feel everything.
Self-validation comes after acceptance.

You might go through the following in the early aftermath of divorce (and sometimes for a considerable amount of time after):

Sadness, hurt, and betrayal
fear, doubt, and uncertainty
distaste and disdain
animosity, rage, or anger
grief, loss, and regret
Peace and relief
loneliness
Internal conflict can frequently be caused by these emotions.

You could experience a great deal of rage, resentment, and grief if your ex-spouse started the divorce because they lost interest in you or met someone else. You might still adore them just as much as you did in the past, though.

You might experience excruciating relief at knowing that your decision to leave an abusive, poisonous, or unhealthy marriage was the right one. But along with this nice sensation of serenity, you might also be feeling a little depressed.

You have the right to feel anything you choose. Even while it might feel overwhelming right now, these feelings will probably pass with time.

While waiting:

Meditation and other mindfulness techniques can improve self-awareness and assist you in making room for all of your emotions, including unpleasant ones. Here's how to develop the practice of everyday meditation.

Do you often get stuck in cycles of unpleasant or negative thoughts? You can control your rumination by using these suggestions.
Having trouble controlling your emotional outbursts? Learn new techniques for controlling your emotions.

Make a co-parenting strategy.
Evidence indicates that when parents work together to share parenting duties with the other parent, children perform better in every way.

Spending at least 35% of the time with each parent led to better emotional, behavioral, and physical health as well as greater connections with both parents, according to a 2014 assessment of 40 studies.
A healthy child's growth and the well-being of the entire family are impacted by keeping a good parenting connection with your ex after divorce, according to studies from the year 2020.

Early planning can reduce disputes over who gets the first pick of the summer vacation, holiday weekends, and other opportunities. Additionally, it can aid in the early development of a courteous communication style.

Try to keep your attention on what's best for your kids rather than on who "wins" or gets the "better deal."

Let's say your ex continues to live in the area where your children already attend school and works from home. Your kids might benefit more from spending a little more time there during the academic year and more time with you during the summer.

Do you co-parent with a toxic or violent ex? The first stage in the process is to seek expert legal and mental health assistance.

A solid co-parenting strategy should contain the following:

plans for spending time with each parent
bedtime, homework, and screen time schedules

Rules and the repercussions of breaching them
household tasks and other obligations
how you'll communicate with the kids when they're living with the other parent
How to inform them about the divorce
In essence, it communicates to your children that even if you no longer live together, you and I still have your best interests in mind.

Remain composed and use assertive communication
You may be upset, angry, and filled with nothing but hatred for your ex. But if you have to stay in touch, it might be helpful to put those emotions on hold for the time being.

That does not mean you should disregard your feelings. Just be careful not to let them influence your talks as you work out the details.

Several useful hints

Set restrictions on communication. Do you plan to phone, text, or email me? How often?
Talk only about what is necessary, such as childcare or any financial arrangements you have made.
Avert jabs, insults, and any other hurtful or sarcastic comments.
Make sure you and your partner have enough time to talk and hear one other out.
Learn more about aggressive communication techniques.

Spend time with your kids being kids.
It can be easier to adjust after a divorce if you make it a point to engage in enjoyable

activities and establish new traditions with your kids.

No matter how hectic and demanding your new daily schedule becomes, set aside sometime each day to check in with your kids and unwind as a family.

You don't need to stray too far from your typical routine or make every moment enjoyable and thrilling. however, you might:

Make time for one enjoyable outing per week, such as a visit to the movies, the beach, or a park.
Create new traditions, such as dinnertime board game play or family supper preparation.
Each night, spend 30 minutes discussing the day's events.
In general, it's best to:

Respond to inquiries in a sincere but age-appropriate manner.

Remain composed and unassuming.
Stay away from making judgmental, harsh, and unpleasant remarks about the other parent.
Keep it factual.
Insisting that relationships don't always work out despite partners' best efforts can also:

Remind your kids that they weren't to blame for the divorce.
build a foundation for healthy relationship skills so that they will know they have the option to leave if they ever find themselves in an unsatisfactory relationship.

Contact your loved ones
You'll probably need some privacy to express any resentment, sadness, or anguish you may be feeling.

Your ability to handle the ongoing stress of the divorce and improve your general well-being can benefit from talking these feelings out with your support network.

Friends and relatives can provide both emotional support and practical answers, such as a place to stay, assistance with childcare, or just considerate advice. They can listen with empathy (and understanding, if they've previously gone through a divorce).

Just keep in mind that you don't need to talk about your emotions with individuals who will judge you or make you feel worse. Make an effort to communicate only with family members who are supportive, sympathetic, and kind.

Think about enlarging your friend network. Sharing our shared possessions is one thing, but what about friends you have in common?

Shared friends frequently lean toward one partner after a divorce rather than the other. You might have "inherited" your spouse's buddies after you got married if you didn't have many friends of your own.

Although it's not usually the case, you may have been close enough that your friendship persists after divorce. When the marriage ends, you could experience feelings of isolation and loneliness.

Making new connections can foster opportunities for social connection and reduce feelings of loneliness.

Here are some pointers for meeting new people:

Participate in community service.
Invite a pleasant coworker to lunch, coffee, or a weekend stroll.
Attend a class in cooking, painting, music, or exercise.

Participate in a divorce support group.

Get back in touch with yourself
Even if you believed you knew yourself rather well, divorce may cause you to reevaluate who you are.

It is undeniable that a relationship may alter a person, and you can find that you are no longer the same person you were before getting married.

Some of your present routines and preferences may have developed organically as a result of your preferences and routines. Others, though, can be a reflection of your ex's requirements and tastes.

Perhaps you'd prefer (or wouldn't prefer):

spend more time outdoors than in a gym.
eat only plant-based foods
live in a constrained space

rather than staying up late and sleeping in, go to bed and wake up early.
Don't forget to take into account your interests and hobbies. After all, your marital leisure activities may not have been consistent with your individual need for rest and solitude.

Making time for self-discovery as you travel your route after a divorce might help you identify important needs and strategies to meet them on your terms.

Test out new techniques
You may have plenty of time to go about hypothetical situations and descend into a cycle of uneasy emotions as a result of the sense of purposelessness that frequently develops the following divorce.

Changing up your routine could help with:

combating loneliness and other undesirable emotions

avoiding the negative behaviors such as ruminating that result from emotional suffering

Nothing inherently wrong with sticking to a tried-and-true regimen. Nevertheless, creating new habits can encourage a feeling of freshness while highlighting the fact that your life is entirely yours.

Several things to think about

Discover happiness in simple rituals, such as taking a break for tea and a nice book on the porch.

Establish a customized self-care routine and make it a daily habit rather than a last-minute consideration.

Make your house or bedroom into a private area for you.

Make sure your bedtime ritual is relaxing.

Make time for yoga, walking, or any other regular, satisfying physical activity.

Don't assign blame.
Most often, a marriage's demise is caused by a variety of causes. Both of your behaviors probably had some impact, unless your relationship was poisonous or abusive (abuse is never your responsibility).

You might find it hard to see things from their point of view right now. However, remembering that people evolve might be beneficial.

When you realize you didn't know each other that well, a star-crossed courtship, a storybook wedding, and a protracted honeymoon phase can all abruptly end. Or perhaps you got married before you had a chance to finish maturing and coming to terms with who you were and what you wanted out of life.

Although communication troubles or incompatibility don't ever justify lying or cheating, they might occasionally shed light on what went wrong and why.

It might not be very helpful for you to go forward to place blame on either yourself or them. Instead, make an effort to adopt a more impartial viewpoint that requires blatantly admitting your contributions. By doing this, you can reduce your rage in the now and foster better connections in the future.

Spend some alone time.
Regarding potential future partnerships, delaying a new connection can be preferable to jumping right into a new one. It may seem that intimacy and love are the best ways to assuage heartache and pass lonely hours. The loss of your marriage hasn't fully healed, though, so beginning a new relationship won't necessarily be beneficial.

You might obtain:

contrasting your current relationship with your ex-partner

finding it challenging to devote the necessary emotional attention to the new relationship

neglecting your demands for physical and emotional wellbeing in favor of those of your new relationship

Undoubtedly, being alone can be frightening, especially if you've never lived alone. However, it is undoubtedly possible to find happiness and contentment on your own.

Use this advice to plunge into living alone.

Work with a qualified person

Your emotional and mental health may be affected by divorce for some time to come, but a mental health expert can always provide understanding advice and support.

A therapist can assist you in investigating coping mechanisms for any distressing or challenging thoughts that surface, such as:

profound and pervasive sorrow
doubt and uncertainty in oneself
sentiments of guilt or failure
severe irritation or anger
depression symptoms
A smoother transition for your family can also be facilitated by a family therapist or co-parenting counselor.

It's always a wise decision to seek out expert assistance if you:

have trouble managing daily activities or parenting your children
find that your performance at work or school has declined
have issues meeting your fundamental requirements like eating, sleeping, or urinating
you start avoiding family members.

Do you require assistance right away?
You're not alone if you're thinking about injuring yourself or taking your own life.

Divorce may result in severe and long-lasting anguish, leaving you feeling helpless and unsure of how to begin feeling better.

Sharing these ideas can be challenging, to put it mildly, but professional crisis counselors are always available to listen with empathy and provide crisis-coping help.

Chapter 6

How to be happy without a partner

One of the biggest misunderstandings many singles have is that getting married or having children will somehow "complete" their lives and make them happier or more fulfilled. The truth? If you already feel content and satisfied on your own, finding romantic fulfillment is far more possible.

At least, such is the conclusion of recent studies. People who were content with their lives had a good attitude and were not depressed before meeting their partners were considerably more likely to report being happy in their relationships, according to one study, which looked at multiple data sets of 11,196 couples.

In other words, attempting to improve your life alone will improve your chances of finding a fulfilling relationship.

Relationship expert Emily Gough argues that when you're content with your own life, you'll only be willing to welcome someone in who is a good fit and brings even more value to your life, rather than getting involved with someone as a substitute for being single.

Because you feel more deserving and self-assured, this effect not only helps you locate a better mate but also enables you to set better limits in your relationships.

You'll also be more likely to attract people who are happy and secure if you radiate those qualities yourself, according to the resident dating expert.

It puts a lot of pressure on both yourself and your new partner to make things work if you anticipate a relationship to make your life better or complete you, the author continues.

So that you're ready to seize the opportunity when the appropriate person enters your life, here are some simple strategies to develop happiness in your life.

How to Enjoy Your Single Life

Put in the arduous healing work
There is no better moment than the present to get on clearing up whatever emotional baggage you may be carrying around, whether it be betrayals from a prior relationship or childhood wounds.

Many people attempt to skip this step, she says, and wind up in unhappy marriages as a result. To be able to accept, receive, or be completely fulfilled in even the best relationship, we must first learn to accept ourselves from the inside out.

When dealing with serious trauma, working with a qualified mental health counselor is ideal. Gough claims that you may also learn a lot from self-help books and podcasts if a therapist is not available to you (or if you simply wish to take a different approach).

Of course, identifying and taking responsibility for your worries, as well as how they can be influencing you and your relationships, is the first step. The next step is to start identifying better coping mechanisms, such as writing, exercise, meditation, or breathing work, that may assist you in overcoming these challenging feelings.

But most importantly, always remember to be kind to yourself. Hurrying the process won't help you, as healing from past hurt might take time.

Put a date on it.
When did you last go on a date with yourself? Did you woo yourself? Have you asked yourself any serious inquiries?

While getting ready to meet a potential companion, CEO of Selective Search and matchmaker Barbie Adler advises all of her clients to "date" themselves.

"Book yourself a solitary trip, if it works within your budget," advises Gough. "You can learn to appreciate the delight of your own company, which will make you realize how valuable your time and attention are to someone else," the author writes. "You'll discover more about yourself and how you relate to the world.

There are many other methods to date yourself even if a solo trip is not currently possible for you.

For instance, there's no need to wait until you have a date before visiting that hip new tapas restaurant or cocktail bar that just opened up nearby. Instead, treat yourself to a meal there now. Write a positive, uplifting note to yourself at night that you can read to yourself in the morning to help you start the day off well.

Lastly, spend some quality time with yourself, whether it be preparing a delicious meal, taking a long walk around your neighborhood, or engaging in creative endeavors. It will be easier for you to be in the appropriate frame of mind when you can spend some time alone with your thoughts and truly enjoy it.

Concentrate on those pastimes
Interested in learning the guitar? It could be time to start taking lessons or simply look at some YouTube courses. Having a sporty void? Go play in a pickup basketball or hockey league.

According to Adler, "love frequently comes into our life while we are joyfully pursuing our hobbies."

These types of hobbies not only provide you the chance to learn skills that will make you more appealing to dates, but they also help you feel more confident about yourself, which will make you appear more desirable to other singles.

Additionally, engaging in activities you enjoy "simply because" brings a feeling of play and enjoyment into your life, which is crucial when navigating the frequently complicated and discouraging world of dating.

Allow time for your buddies

Focusing on strengthening the relationships you currently have is considered by experts to be one of the top things single people can do to improve their chances of finding love.

Before meeting a romantic partner, developing friendships with like-minded people can significantly increase your pleasure and contentment.

Uncertain about how to meet new people? Use your smartphone right away. According to research from Plenty of Fish, singles are placing a higher priority on utilizing and growing their singles networks. In fact, according to 69% of singles, dating apps are just as effective at connecting people with shared interests as they are at finding partners for romantic relationships, and 59% of singles claim to have made new friends through dating apps in the past two years.

A solid community can help make dating less stressful and more enjoyable so that you can enjoy getting to know someone without feeling rushed, according to Maclean.

Get rid of anything that is no longer useful to you.

Marlena Del Hierro, a life coach, and relationship coach advise singles to engage in "radical self-care," which is consciously deciding to prioritize your needs. Del Hierro asserts that as part of that practice, you might have to do rid of some routines, behaviors, or even people who aren't supporting your needs and general wellbeing.

For instance, it's probably time to adjust your sleep schedule and nighttime routine if staying up late to binge Netflix prevents you from exercising in the morning or from being your best self at work.

You could also want to limit your time with them and find someone new to hang out with if one of your close pals has a negative attitude that you find tiring or harmful to your outlook.

Spending time with people who uplift and inspire you, who may or may not be your present group of friends, is a component of radical self-care, according to Del Hierro. If you're unhappy with your current position or the working environment, it may be necessary to change it.

Taking all of these actions can significantly improve your level of pleasure and satisfaction in life, and who knows? "The One" may appear just as you begin to understand that you don't need anyone else to be happy. Whatever happens, according to Gough, the important thing is to live a life you're passionate about because, if you do, you could run into someone who is as well.